Landing i

CW01467299

AUS
Billabong
G'day!
AUS
AUS
Australia
travel to
AUSTRALIA
AUS
Aussie
Hooroo!
AUS

Getting an Australian SIM Card (Updated March 2023)

With International roaming often costing the earth and a family back home wanted to know you have arrived and are safe, buying an Aussie SIM is often the first priority.

In Australia there are three mobile network owners/operators: Telstra, Optus and Vodafone.

All other mobile service providers (MVNO) lease services from one of these three networks.

Population Coverage

Telstra   - *99.5%*
Optus   - *98.5%*
Vodafone - *96%*

Don't be fooled....

The networks only need to cover the populated areas of Australia to meet the figures listed above, but there are a lot of unpopulated areas that get no coverage at all. Check out each network's geographic coverage here:

whistleout.com.au/MobilePhones/Guides/who-has-the-best-mobile-coverage

Mobile Virtual Network Operators

There are many other smaller mobile phone plan providers called Mobile Virtual Network Operators (MVNO). They all operate through one of the above 3 networks. Customers on the 'big three' networks get full access to everything those networks have to offer. MVNO customers may be limited to certain parts of the network. Some of the MVNOs are listed below:

TELSTRA	OPTUS	VODAPHONE
ALDIMobile	amaysim	felix mobile
Belong Mobile	Aussie Broadband	iiNet
Boost Mobile	Catch Connect	Internode
Exetel	Circles.Life	Kogan Mobile
Lycamobile	Coles Mobile	Lebara Mobile
Mate	Dodo	TPG
numobile	Gomo	
Tangerine Telecom	iPrimus	
Woolworths Mobile	Moose Mobile	
	Southern Phone	
	SpinTel	
	Yomojo	

Pre-Paid SIM cards (Pay As You Go) can be purchased from Network Stores, Airports, Post Offices, News Agencies, Supermarkets and some Electronic Stores.

HINT** Boost mobile is a MVNO with access to the full Telstra network.

So, which network?

Telstra	Of the three networks, Telstra has the best reputation and they may be the best choice for travellers visiting regional and remote areas, however they are also famous for being the most expensive!
Optus	Generally good coverage in major cities but more limited in rural areas. Good deals reasonably $$$.
Vodaphone	Often cheapest of the 'big three', coverage can be very limited outside of major cities, depending on the area.

CALLING/MESSAGING OVERSEAS

To call overseas from Australia, you'll need to dial the **exit code**, the **country code** and the **phone number** (and area code, if you are calling a landline).

Exit code of Australia ____ + or **0011**

Drop the '0'

Once you have entered *Australia's Exit code* and the *International Country code* of where you are trying to call, next comes the *Area code* (if calling a landline) or the *Mobile number*.
If the Area code or Mobile number starts with a 0 then leave it off.

EXAMPLE;

If you are calling someone in the UK and their phone number in the UK is 07816 190 192;

Dial
(1) the exit code to call outside Australia **+ or 00 11**
(2) the country code for the UK **44**
7816 190 192
notice the '0' at the start has been dropped

4

HAVING TROUBLE????

• If the call does not connect, you may have international restrictions active on your account. Contact your network provider and they will be able to help you remove these.

• If you are calling from another country to Australia then you must have international roaming active. To add or remove this, contact your network provider.

• In some countries a successful connection requires that your phone number is shown to the receiver.

Ask you network provider if this is active.

• Running out of credit fast? Consider getting an International Calling Card.

INTERNATIONAL CALLING CARDS

If you are looking to make low-cost international calls to countries around the world, calling cards can be one the cheapest ways to do this. Calling cards are available from most Newsagencies/ Convenience Stores and once purchased they are charged at the rate of a local call. There are many different International Calling cards available so check the rates of the back of the cards to see which one offers the cheapest rate to the country you are trying to call.

OPENING AN BANK

There are many different banks throughout Australia, although currently the biggest 4 are:

- *Australia and New Zealand Banking Group (ANZ)*
- *Commonwealth Bank (CBA)*
- *National Australia Bank (NAB)*
- *WESTPAC*

To open up a bank account you will need;

- a valid passport
- a valid visa
- an additional form of I.D.

Please note: Some banks require additional identification once you have been in the country more than 6 weeks so it's worth opening up your bank account as soon as you arrive!

AUSTRALIAN ACCOUNT

ATM CHARGES

Using another banks ATM will occur a charge of between $2 & $4 per transaction. You may even be charged this fee just to check your account balance. Using a bank's own ATM is free. When choosing a bank look at both the interest rates and do an online map search of each banks ATM locations to see which bank best suits your travelling needs.

Post offices

Australia Post allows you to withdraw and deposit from over 70 different banks with no transaction fee.

Important note **This service is no long available with ANZ accounts.

Please note: Australia Post service is 'over the counter' and most Post offices are closed at weekends and on Public Holidays

➰ auspost.com.au/money-insurance/transfer-money/bank-at-post

CREDIT/SAVINGS/
WHAT'S THE DIFFERENCE?

Whenever you make a purchase or ATM withdrawal in Australia using a card you will have to choose which of the following options suits you best. *So, what's the difference?*

Cheque

A cheque account is traditionally your transactional everyday account. Transactions are processed immediately and funds must be available in your account for you to make the purchase. There is normally no limit on the amount of transactions per month. These accounts generally offer a very low interest rate or no interest rate at all.

Credit

Credit is essentially borrowing money from your card provider up to the limit of your overdraft. This differs from Cheque and Savings (debit accounts) where you must have available funds first. As the funds belong to the bank, you may be charged a surcharge per transaction by the merchant to use your credit card. These additional charges can quickly add up and there may be high fees to consider + interest on outstanding balances.

Savings

This account is designed for stashing your cash! The interest rate may be higher but you may be limited to a certain number of transactions per month or have to deposit a certain amount each month in order to benefit from the better interest rates. This account is great to store funds that you only need to access in an emergency. If you do not have a linked savings account then funds will simply be taken from your cheque account. Just like a cheque account, transactions are processed immediately and funds must be available in your account for you to make the purchase.

CHEQUE/TAP & GO?

Tap and Go

- If your Tap and Go card is a debit card, the funds used for your purchase will come from your transactional account (Cheque) or linked Savings account.
- If your Tap and Go card is a credit card or can be used as a credit card, money for your purchase will be drawn from your credit card account, even if there is also a transactional or savings account linked to your card.

Did you bring a bank cards from overseas?
Debit Card – select *'CHEQUE'*
Credit Card – select *'CREDIT'*

SECURITY AND FRAUD

Credit cards and debit cards generally offer a zero-liability policy. This means you will be refunded for fraudulent transactions.

Credit

One key advantage that credit cards offer in comparison to debit cards is that if there is fraud on your account, it won't affect your actual bank balance or savings meaning you may not be out of pocket while your bank investigates. Credit cards come with fraud-monitoring services and they are generally very vigilant on spotting fraudulent activity.

Debit - Cheque/ Savings

Many debit cards also come with fraud-monitoring services, however, if your debit account is used for fraud, you may be left without that money until the bank has fully investigated the claim. This could take a few weeks or months.

Medicare and Private Health Care

Medicare is the name given to the publicly funded health care system in Australia. It gives Australian residents access to free or subsidised treatment in both public hospitals and by health professionals.

There are currently **11 countries t**hat participate in a **Reciprocal Health Care Agreement (RHCA)** with Australia, however what is covered varies depending on which of these countries you are from. Residents of other countries must pay all medical expenses. Having access to Medicare means you can get help with the cost of essential medical care whilst you are in Australia. You are only entitled once you have applied, so if you are listed below visit Medicare as soon as you arrive… just in case!

If you are from one of the following 11 countries then visit the link below to find out exactly what you are entitled to:

Belgium	New Zealand
Finland	Norway
Italy	Slovenia
Republic of Ireland	Sweden
Malta	United Kingdom
Netherlands	

humanservices.gov.au/rhca

Ambulance Cover

It is important to note that Medicare does **NOT** cover ambulance services or emergency transportation to hospital. The cost for this varies State by State. To avoid these costs, you may wish to consider health ensurance. To find out the ambulance cost for each state, check out the link below.

privatehealth.gov.au/health_insurance/what_is_covered/ ambulance.htm

Private Health Insurance in Australia
Overseas Visitors Health Cover (OVHC)
Overseas Student Health Cover (OSHC)

If your visa requires you to have private health cover and you are not eligible for Medicare then you must purchase either OVHC and OSHC from an Australian-registered health insurer or your visa may not be granted.

If your visa requires you to have private health cover and you are eligible for Medicare then you must check the exact requirements of your visa and make sure that meet the minimum health care cover rules. Even if you are not required to have OVHC or OSHC then it may still be worth considering for the areas that Medicare doesn't cover, such as emergency transportation, dental and optical.

If your visa does not require you to have private health cover then you may prefer to opt for Travel Insurance or take the risk with no cover. If you have Travel Insurance then you need to find out exactly what you are covered for and whether there is an excess (out of pocket expense) to pay. Check emergency transportation and find out whether your insurer pays directly or if you have to pay first and claim back later. Remember if you have no health cover then you could be facing huge medical expenses if you are in an accident or hospitalised whilst in Australia.

How to get a
Medicare Card?

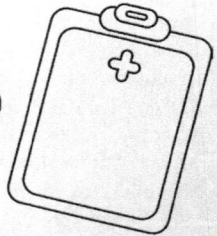

1. Visit the web address below, open the Medicare enrolment form, fill it in, print and sign it.

⇨ *humanservices.gov.au/individuals/forms/ms004*

2. To enrol you need to visit a service centre with a completed Medicare enrolment form and documents you need to show.

For documents you need to show, refer to information under your country at the following web address and scroll to the bottom of the page;

⇨ *humanservices.gov.au/rhca*

If you receive treatment before you have had a change to register, you can apply
Your benefit starts the day you arrived in Australia.

General opening hours
Monday – Friday
8.30am – 4.30pm

To find your nearest Medicare Service Centre visit:

findus.servicesaustralia.gov.au

Medicare general enquiries
7 days a week / 24 hours a day
Call: **132 011**

Contact Medicare from outside Australia
Monday to Friday
9am – 5pm AEST
Call: **+61 2 8633 3284**
International call charges apply

Stay Safe and Healthy

myGov Account

myGov is the online system that allows you to log into government sites such as Medicare, Australian TAX Office (ATO) and My Health Record. You MUST have a myGov account or you will not be able to access your personal information on these sites.

How to set up a MyGov account

You will need to complete the following steps;

Visit *www.my.gov.au* and click **'Create an account'**. You will need an email address that you have access to, to complete the setup process.

Follow the prompts and a security password will be sent to the email address you have provided. You will need to enter this into the myGov setup page to progress to the next step.

Enter an Australian mobile phone number and a confirmation code will be sent to the number you have provided. You will need to enter the code into the myGov setup page to progress. If you do not have an Australian mobile phone number then you can select *'skip this step'*.

Next set up a password that must have at least 7 characters and include at least 1 number.

You will then be prompted to create 3 security questions that only you know the answers to.

Your set up is complete.

How to Log on to myGov?

- Enter your username and password — if you do not have one, follow the steps above to set up a myGov account or follow the link to reset your username and/or password.

- You will be then be prompted to enter a code generated from the app 'myGov Access'. This can be downloaded onto your phone from the Google Play Store or Apple Store.

- If you do not have access to the 'myGov Access' app, a one-time code can be sent to your Australian mobile number.

- If you do not have your phone then you can answer the secret questions.

IMPORTANT:
The FIRST TIME you access your myGov account, go to 'ACCOUNT SETTINGS' and select 'SIGN IN OPTIONS'. Select the sign in method that works for you but remember if you do not select 'Answer a secret question' you will not be able to access your account at all without your Australian mobile phone number or the 'myGov Access' app already set up.

To contact the myGov helpdesk;

From Australia
Call **13 23 07**, *select Option 1*

From outside Australia
Call **+61 1300 1MYGOV (1300 169 468)**, *select Option 1*

Opening Hours:

7:00am - 10:00pm
Monday - Friday

&

10:00am - 5:00pm
Saturday - Sunday
in local Australian time zones.

ID Cards

When you check in at many backpacker hostels throughout Australia, you will need to hand over your passport for the duration of your stay. This is common practice, but may leave you without a form of ID that you will need if you are heading out for a beer.

Why do I need an ID card?

- As an alternative form of ID to a passport or a driver licence.
- To increase the number of IDs you own to make it easier when applying for services.
- To avoid damaging or losing your passport or driver licence.

Listed below are all the direct links to Australia Post and State specific ID card applications and forms.

Australia Post Keypass 18+ ID Card
auspost.com.au/id-and-document-services/apply-for-a-keypass-id

Keypass in Digital iD™
With Keypass in Digital iD™ you're able to use your smartphone to prove your age, so that you can purchase alcohol and gain entry to 18+ venues.
digitalid.com/personal

State specific ID Cards

New South Wales Photo Card
⇨ *service.nsw.gov.au/transaction/apply-for-a-nsw-photo-card*

Queensland Photo Identification Card
⇨ *qld.gov.au/transport/licensing/proof-of-age*

Western Australia Photo Card
⇨ *transport.wa.gov.au/licensing/photo-card.asp*

South Australia Proof of Age Card
⇨ *sa.gov.au/topics/driving-and-transport/licences/proof-of-age-card*

Tasmania Personal Information Card
⇨ *service.tas.gov.au/services/me-and-my-identity/personal-information-card/apply-for-renew-or-replace-a-personal-information-card*

ACT Proof of Identity Card
⇨ *accesscanberra.act.gov.au/s/article/proof-of-identity-cards-tab-overview*

Northern Territory Evidence of Age Card
⇨ *nt.gov.au/driving/mvr-services/apply-for-nt-evidence-of-age-card*

Working Holiday Visa

If you want to work whilst backpacking around Australia, you'll need to apply for a Working Holiday (subclass 417) visa or Work and Holiday (subclass 462) visa.

Basic Eligibility

- Must be 18 to 30 years old (inclusive) - except for Canadian and Irish citizens up to 35 (inclusive)

- Must have a passport from an eligible country that is involved in the Working Holiday Program with Australia

- Must not be accompanied by dependent children

> *A working holiday visa lets you work for up to one year in Australia. Typically, you can only work for an individual employer for up to 6 months. However, if the work takes place in different locations, it is sometimes possible to work for the same employer in Australia for an entire year.*
>
> An Australian working holiday visa is available to overseas passport holders from countries with which Australia has a reciprocal agreement.

Visa subclass 417

Belgium	Finland	Italy	Norway
Canada	France	Japan	Sweden
Cyprus	Germany	South Korea	Taiwan
Denmark	Hong Kong	Malta	United Kingdom
Estonia	Ireland	Nederlands	

Visa subclass 462

Argentina	Indonesia	Portugal	Thailand
Austria	Israel	San Marino	Turkey
Chile	Luxembourg	Singapore	United States
China	Malaysia	Slovakia	Uruguay
Czech Republic	Peru	Slovenia	Vietnam
Hungary	Poland	Spain	

A Working Holiday (subclass 417) visa or Work and Holiday (subclass 462) visa is granted for 12 months with the option applying for a second visa after completing 3 months specified work in rural Australia

> "From 1 July 2019, WHM visa holders who carry out 3 months of specified work in regional areas while on their second Working Holiday (subclass 417) visa or Work and Holiday (subclass 462) visa may be eligible to apply for a third visa. Eligible types of work and regional areas will correspond with the requirements for the second visa."

Government, I. (2019, April 10). Working Holiday Visa. Retrieved from Department of Home Affairs Immigration and Citizenship:

immi.homeaffairs.gov.au/visas/getting-a-visa/visa-listing/work-holiday-417

TAX FILE NUMBER (TFN)

If you have a visa that allows you to work in Australia or if you intend to keep money in an Australian Bank account then it is important that you apply for a Tax File Number (TFN)

Your TFN is your personal reference number for the Australian Tax and Superannuation systems and it is free to apply. The TFN is yours for life and you will need this to claim back any Tax or Superannuation payments you have made during your trip, once you permanently leave Australia so KEEP IT SAFE!

To apply for your TFN online visit the ATO (Australian Taxation Office) at the web address below:

ato.gov.au/individuals/tax-file-number/

Once you have your Tax File Number you will need to link it to a MyGov account. This will allow you to view how much you have paid in tax and superannuation contributions whilst in Australia and make it a lot simpler to claim this back when you leave. *(see p. 14-15)*

Bogans True Blue Guide to Chin Wagging With Cobbers   A – B

Avo	Avocado	Avo on toast.
Arvo/ S'arvo	Afternoon, this afternoon	I'm going to the shops s'arvo.
Bail/ Bailed	Cancelled plans, leaving	Sarah has bailed. I'm going to bail.
Barbie	Barbeque, BBQ	Let's have a barbie on Saturday.
Bathers	Swimming attire	Don't forget to pack your bathers.
Beaut/ Beauty	Brilliant, fantastic, great	I won? You beauty!
Billabong	An isolated pond left behind after a river changes course	Let's cool our feet in the billabong.
Billy	A metal pot with lid used for making tea or cooking	All I took camping was my swag and my billy.
Bloody	Used to emphasis a point	It was bloody brilliant.
Bloody oath	Yes or true	You right mate? Bloody Oath.
Bludger	Someone who is lazy or expects others to do stuff for them	Get off ya bum ya bludger!
Bogan	Uncultured person with unrefined speech, behaviour, clothing. Often found drinking beer	Look at that group of bogans!
Bonza	Great	That's bonza mate!
Bottle – O	Bottle Shop, Liquor Store	I'm just heading to the bottle-o.
Brisvegas	Affectionate name for Brisbane	I'm going to Brisvegas for the weekend.
Budgie Smugglers	Speedos, men's swimming briefs/trunks	Those budgie smugglers don't cover much!
Bush	Australian countryside, usually one that is heavily forested and sparsely populated	Did you have fun camping out bush?"

Cont. on page 29

Dorm Living

For many, backpacking just wouldn't be backpacking without hostels and of course dorm rooms! Sharing your sleeping quarters with strangers can seem a bit daunting at first but you soon get use to it and if you follow the 'dorm room etiquette' you will be making friends and loving dorm life in no time.

Be friendly and smile

First impressions can make all the difference. Even if you are exhausted after a big journey, making the effort to smile, say 'hi' and using your manners goes a long way with your fellow backpackers. Even if there is a language barrier, everyone appreciates a warm smile.

Be considerate of your roommates

The experience of being a backpacker is unique to everyone and it is likely that some of the people you are sharing with will have totally different schedules to you. Some will party, some will work and some want to do yoga on the beach at 5am. Daytime naps are common so be considerate at all times.

Be organised

If you need to be up early or you know you will be coming back late then get everything ready during the day. Pack all your bags and just leave out your toiletries. If you are arriving at a hostel late at night, then get ready for bed in one of the communal bathrooms before entering your dorm room. If you need to set an alarm get up as soon as it goes off.

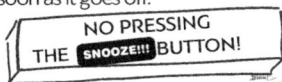

NO PRESSING THE SNOOZE!!! BUTTON!

Don't turn the lights on at night

If you need to get up in the night use a torch. Your phone has one but they can be just as bright as the main room light! Invest in a small keyring light or use the screen light on your phone to navigate to the door.

Don't borrow your roommate's things

Even if you don't think they will mind, you must ASK FIRST! These are people's personal possessions and even if it wouldn't bother you if someone plugs their phone into your charger or borrows a bit of milk from the room fridge, it can upset even the most chilled out backpacker. ASK, ASK and if in doubt **ASK!**

Can I ...?

Technology after lights out

If you want to watch a movie or play games on your phone or tablet, then go to the common areas. Even with the screen brightness down low, it can be very bright in a pitch black room and no one likes being woken up in the middle of the night. Make sure your phone is on silent and definitely no calls.... Not even at a whisper!

Invest in sleeping aids

Just because you are being considerate, doesn't guarantee everyone else will be. Investing in some earplugs and a sleeping mask can avoid lots of sleepless nights and angry conversations. They are also great for long bus rides or daytime catch up naps. Remember as annoying as it can be, no one can help snoring and if you are a snorer then mention it to your roommates so that they have the opportunity to invest in some earplugs themselves!

Keep your part of the room tidy

Remember you are not at home! Keep your part of the room tidy by making your bed and keeping all your belongings together. Bunk beds are for sleeping, not for hanging your washing out to dry!

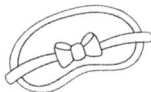

Bathroom rush hours

Some hostels have communal bathrooms and some have a bathroom for each dorm room. Either way, you will find there is a rush hour first thing in the morning and last thing at night with frustrated backpackers queuing to use the showers. Often the bathrooms are deserted during the day so if you can, wait. If you have to use the bathrooms during rush hour, then keep showers short and sweet. It is a great idea to wear flip flops (thongs) in the bathrooms and showers as the floors are not always the most hygienic of places to walk around barefoot!

Keep the noise down

Let's make this perfectly clear... hanging a sheet off of the side of your bunk bed and getting amorous with a fellow backpacker in a dorm room is never ok.

It DOES NOT reduce noise, rocking or creaking! If you can't keep your hands off each other then go somewhere else or combine funds and invest in a private room for the night. Ignore this advice at your own peril or you will have to face some very upset roommates in the morning!

Get involved in Hostel Life/ Promotions

This is a great way to connect with fellow backpackers and have some fun. Ask at reception if they have any weekly promotions or events coming up so that you can add them into your schedule. It's also a great icebreaker to ask around and see who else will be going. These events and promos often involve discounts so it's also a great way to save money and get the most out of your backpacking experience.

Label food

Hostels have communal fridges and some dorm rooms have small bar fridges. Either way, make sure your food is clearly labelled. Anything not marked clearly with your name and room number will be thrown away by the cleaners or taken by other backpackers.

Communal kitchens and washing up

When using the communal kitchens then it's important to understand that cooking equipment is limited. If you are cooking, then make sure you wash up for the next person BEFORE eating your meal and don't leave plates in the sink. Due to the amount of cutlery/ crockery that gets stolen, many hostels give you a set in exchange for a deposit that you get back once everything is returned at the end of your stay. Keep all the items safe as you will be charged for any items not returned.

Communicate

Communication is key! If something or someone is bothering you, address it calmly before it turns into a big deal. Often the person involved is completely oblivious that they are even causing an issue and a friendly conversation can save a huge argument at a later date. Remember no one is perfect. If that doesn't rectify the problem, then speak to the hostel staff rather than bad mouthing the person in question to anyone that will listen. They may be able to move you to another room. It's easy to make friends if you are fun, approachable and willing to put yourself out there. You won't regret it and you might end up with lifelong friendships!

Living Cheap

Travelling on a budget is a skill that improves the more you do it. Here are some simple tips that will help you save money for the more important things in life... like having fun!

FREE WIFI AREAS

All major cities have free WiFi areas ranging from cafes, fast food chains, airports, shopping centres, tourist attractions, libraries and even some beaches! Ask locals and fellow backpackers around the area and share your backpacking experiences online there rather than using up all your precious mobile data.

Plan ahead and book packages

Booking your tours as a package is often a HUGE money saver. Take the time to plan ahead so that the trips you are booking have availability that suits your schedule. Many hostels are also travel agents and they look after their guests. If you are staying in a hostel, go and see the front desk today and discuss what you would like to experience around Australia. They have first-hand knowledge of the trips and won't just sell you whatever gets them the best commission!

Eating out is often cheaper for lunch than dinner

If you want to experience the local cuisine, keep a look out for 'Lunchtime Specials' as these are often a lot cheaper, especially during the week.

Cooking

Cooking for yourself is the cheapest way to eat, even fast food can be quite pricey. Grocery shopping costs can however soon add up and often you will have way more food than you need due to the packet sizes. To avoid eating minute noodles every day, try teaming up with fellow travellers and making something in bulk to share like spaghetti bolognaise or a stir fry. Your body will love you for it and it's a great way to make new friends.

The 2 biggest supermarket chains in Australia are Woolworths and Coles.

BBQ

No trip to Australia would be complete without a Barbie (BBQ). It's a great way to get out in the fresh air and with free gas BBQs in most of the major parks in Australia, it doesn't need to be expensive! Grab a loaf of bread, some sausages and some sauce *(see FREE FOOD SHELF)* and you are good to go!

FREE FOOD SHELF

Most hostels have a free food shelf where backpackers leave any unwanted food when the move onto their next destination. It's a great place to pick up sauces, seasonings, oil, pasta, canned goods etc and can save you a lot of cash at the supermarkets.

Bottle shops

The cost of alcohol can vary a lot between different bottle shops and in some remote areas and small towns the cost can be insane. Plan ahead and if necessary, buy in a major city rather than waiting to get to your destination. Ask about for the cheapest place to buy. Even if it only saves you a few $$$ it all adds up. *(See GOON)*

GOON

The cheapest alcohol to drink is GOON. It looks like a boxed wine but don't be fooled! It is in fact a fish, dairy, and milk product that tastes like a bad wine. It gets you very drunk and is famous for giving most people a horrible hangover. However, almost every backpacker in Australia has experienced a night out on the goon at some point so don't fight trying it too much!

Laundry mate

Doing your laundry can be quite expensive and if you are travelling alone it can be hard to fill the washing machine with things to wash. Try finding yourself a laundry mate so that you can share the expense and you only need half a load each. Plus, less loads means its better for the environment too!

Blow up the empty goon bag for a pillow on the go!

Bogans True Blue Guide to Chin Wagging With Cobbers   C – G

Cactus	Dead	The car is cactus!
Carked	Dead	The car has carked it!
Chips	Crisps, hot chip = chips	I'm going to the cafe for some hot chips.
Chook	Chicken	Let's get a hot chook from the supermarket.
Cobber	Mate	G'day, cobber!
Coldie	Beer	Are you coming to the pub for a coldie?
Cozzie	Swimming costume	Don't forget to pack your cozzie!
Crikey	Used as an exclamation	Crikey! Look at that snake!
Crook	Feeling unwell	I feel crook.
Dag	Geek, nerd	You are such a dag!
Daks	Trousers	Pull up your daks, I can see your crack.
Deadset	True	You are a deadest legend.
Devo	Devastated	I am totally devo.
Drongo	Idiot	Stop being such a drongo.
Dunny	Toilet	Does anyone need the dunny?
Esky	Australian brand of portable coolers	Can you grab me a beer from the esky?
Fair dinkum	Real or seriously?	Fair dinkum, the fish I caught was huge!
Footy	Could refer to AFL, Rugby League or Rugby Union	Did ya watch the footy last night.
G'Day	Hello	G'Day mate.
Galah	Idiot	You're a flaming galah.
Gnarly	Surfing term difficult, challenging or dangerous	Dude that wave was gnarly!
Goon	Cheap boxed wine alternative	My head hurts after drinking all that goon!

Cont. on page 30

Bogans True Blue Guide to Chin Wagging With Cobbers H – T

Hard yakka	Hard work	*He has certainly put in the hard yakka.*
Larrikin	A mischievous young person	*He is lively, energetic and a bit of a larrikin.*
Lollies	Sweets of all kinds	*I'm going to get a bag of lollies.*
Manchester	Linen, tablecloths	*I need to go to the Manchester department to get new sheets.*
Middy	Another name for a pot glass	*Can I have a middy of beer please.*
No wakkas	Abbreviation of 'no worries'	*Can you help me? No wakkas!*
No worries	No problem	*Thanks for your help. No worries mate!*
Outback	Inland Australia. More remote than the bush	*She went solo backpacking in the Australian Outback.*
Pash	A kiss generally with tongues!	*I pashed a total hottie last night.*
Pommy	An English person	*Are you bringing your pommy girlfriend?*
Pot	285ml drinking glass	*Can I have a pot of beer please?*
Rack off	Go away	*Will you just rack off.*
Rapt	Delighted, happy, fully engrossed in something	*I am rapted I caught that sic wave.*
Ripper	Something excellent	*Your surf boards a ripper.*
Root	To have sex with	*Did you root that hottie last night?*
Rooted	Broken or tired	*I am so rooted after that night out.*
Runners	Trainers or sneakers	*Bring your runners for the gym.*
Sanger	Sandwich	*Let's have sausage sangers at the bbq.*

Schooner	425ml drinking glass (except in SA is 285ml)	Can I have a schooner of beer please?
Servo	Petrol station, service station	Do you want anything else from the servo?
'She'll be right'	It will all turn out ok	Don't worry, she'll be right mate!
Sheep shagger	New Zealander	Are you an Aussie or a sheep shagger?
Shelia	Woman	Look at that smokin' hot Shelia!
Sick/ sic	Really great	That wave was sic!
Slab	24 pack of beer	I'm going to the bottle-o to get a slab of beer.
Snag	Sausage	Lets put some snags on the barbie.
Spewin'	Not happy, upset, angry	I was spewin' I didn't come first.
Stoked	Happy, exited, exhilarated	I am stoked I caught that wave.
Straya	Australia	I love Straya!
Strewth	An exclamation of surprise	Strewth it's hot today!
Stubby	A bottle of beer typically holding 375ml	Pass me a stubby mate!
Stubby holder	A sleeve or cylinder designed to insulate a beverage	Can I use that stubby holder? My beer is getting warm!
Swag	A portable sleeping unit used by travellers in the bush	I'm not taking a tent, just my swag.
Tinny	A small aluminium boat	Fancy taking the tinny out?
Thongs	Flip flops	Don't forget your thongs at the beach.
Togs	Swimming attire	I can't go swimming without my togs!
True Blue	Real	You are a true-blue Aussie!
Tucker	Food	I'm hungry, its time to get some tucker.
Two Up	A traditional Australian gambling game only legal on Anzac day	Let's go to the pub for a game of two up!

Cont. on page 37

How to get around

Australia is the world's biggest island (@ 7.962 million km^2) so the way you travel and the cost of travel needs careful consideration so that you have money left to spend on the important things like having fun!

Buses and Coaches

Still one of the most popular modes of transport for backpackers and tourists alike, buses and coach companies offer a huge variety of different ticketing options from single trip fares to fully inclusive multi-day travel with guides. 'Hop-on, Hop-off' tickets are very popular as they give you flexibility to adjust your itinerary without being out of pocket. Talk to your hostel travel agent and they will help you choose a company and ticket option that works best for your planned itinerary and budget. Most long-distance buses/coaches have aircon and WIFI.

Internal Flights

There are now 5 main domestic airline companies. Qantas Domestic, Jetstar (subsidiary of Qantas), Virgin Australia and Rex (who operates in regional Australia too) have been around for a long time. Bonza is the newest domestic airline company, launched in early 2023 and is making a name for itself as one of the big players. Flights can be very expensive but if you are short of time, they can be an excellent way to get from A to B quickly. For cheaper fares,

Australia?

Catch a lift

Backpackers who own or rent vehicles regularly want passengers to fill empty seats to make the trip more fun and to help share fuel costs. One of the best places to look is your hostel notice board which is always a wealth of information. There is also a host of websites that are dedicated to sharing a ride that can be found with a simple internet search.

the trick is to book early and look for deals. Some airlines offer cheaper fares on a certain day of the week but they don't last long so you will need to be quick! A great way to look for flights is to go to a flight comparison website, then contact the airline directly so that you are not paying unnecessary commission. For Bonza flights, book direct through their app.

Buying a car

This can be a great way to travel around and if you're able to split the fuel costs it can be very cost effective. However, **this can be very risky if you don't have adequate mechanical knowledge**. Breaking down in the middle of nowhere can be pretty scary and being rescued or your car being repaired can be very expensive. If you know what you are doing then you should be able to pick up a car for a few thousand dollars and you have the option of selling it at the end of your trip. Hostel notice boards in major cities are a great way to find cars as well as searching the internet in your area.

Relocation Deals

Campervan and car hire companies often have to relocate vehicles around Australia and rather than paying drivers to do it they offer hugely discounted rates to customers who can do this one-way trip for them. Search 'Relocation deals Australia' and you will find many companies offering these deals. Often you will only have a few days to drive vehicle to its destination so there isn't much time for site seeing but if you need to get up or down the coast fast then this could be a great cheap option.

Travel Card

All major cities have their own version of an electronic travel card that you top up and can be used for trains, buses, ferry, trams and more.

It's often cheaper to use an electronic travel card than to purchase paper tickets and look out for special rates and discounts throughout the year that can add up to big savings.

Hire a Campervan

There are heaps of campervan hire companies that operate out of all the major cities and cater for every type of clientele, from absolute budget to high end campers with all the bells and whistles. Campers can be an excellent way to travel around Australia as it gives you the freedom to go where you want (no beach driving though!) and the cost of your bed is included in the price. You will need to factor in the extra fuel you will go through, due to the extra weight and ensure that you read the terms & conditions and insurance details very carefully and understand the out of pocket expenses if something happens. Find the campervan hire companies in your area and read the reviews!

Trains

Each state offers its own version of a rail pass that is available to International travellers only and are worth checking out. Although travelling by rail can be expensive, if you are travelling solo and planned to drive, it can work out to be cheaper to catch the train once you factor in fuel, hidden costs etc. It is also one of the most relaxing ways to travel. If you are looking for a truly unique experience that allows you to see almost every type of terrain Australia has to offer, check out the incredible train rides below.

Australia boasts many rail experiences including 2 of the worlds most iconic that covers huge distances.

The Ghan   Adelaide - Alice Springs - Darwin
(2979km)

Indian Pacific   Sydney – Adelaide – Perth
(4343km)

Hitch hiking

Yes, it can be a free way to travel, but it can be dangerous. In Queensland and Victoria, it is illegal to hitch-hike from a road, road shoulder, median strip or traffic island. Australia-wide it is illegal to hitchhike on motorways (where pedestrians are prohibited and where cars are not allowed to stop). If you decide to hitchhike then understand the risks and put measures in place to stay safe. Females are statistically more at risk than males and don't try to hitchhike at night. Message friends with as much info as possible (make/ model/ numberplate/ drivers' name/ location/ destination etc) whenever you are offered a lift. Follow your gut. If something doesn't feel right then don't get in the car.

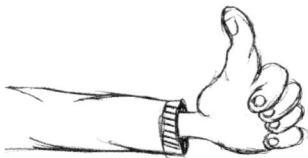

Free Camping

There are many free camping sites around Australia and a simple internet search will help you find them. Some are notoriously difficult to find so plan ahead and work out where you are heading in case you find yourself out of mobile network range. There are books and apps dedicated to free camping that cover the whole of Australia but beware, most free camping spots have very limited or no amenities so it is very unlikely you will get to have a hot shower after a long day driving or exploring.

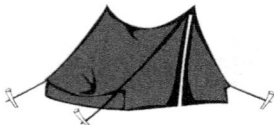

Bogans True Blue Guide to Chin Wagging With Cobbers W – Z

Walkabout   An aboriginal walking trip through bush (generally)

Yarra has gone walkabout.

Woop woop   In the middle of nowhere

I was out the back of woop woop.

Yous   You (usually more than one person)

Are yous still going to the part?

Bird
G'Day
Crook
Shelia
Hooroo
Bloody
Blowie
Banana
Dunny Daks
Footy Tinny
Fair
oath
Cook
Reckon
Tucker
Black
Crack
Beer
Esky
Veg
Dag
Cab
Pash
Spewin
Fisho Outback
Ocker
Brass
Chuck
Mozzie
Dinky-di
Bludger Ute
Doova lacky
Chrissie
Barbie Deadset sickie
Crikey Bender
worries Smoko
Walkabout
Captain
Coldie
crows Cut
Digger
Good
Stump
Stone
Beaut
Blooming
Cooee
Bloke
onya
Damper Bonza heck
Chunder Bogan fight
Strewth
Billabong
Big note
Yumbuck Oi
Bingle pointers
Dead
razoo
Fluid
Whinge
Thongs
Grouse
Mob
horse
dinkum
Nipper
Corker
Aussie
Battler
Larrikin
Bourke
White
Galah Copper
lunch
Slab
Bush
Sav
Yakka
Durry
Amber
Chewie
Moolah
Mate
Troppo
Bunyip
Swag

Travel Notes: _____

Source: Original photo from Flickr User:
Image modified by Landing in Australia

PLOT YOUR TRIP

color line www.creativecommons.org/licenses/by/2.0/legalcode

Driving in Australia

Can I drive in Australia?

If your licence is not in English you will need to get an International Driving Permit (IDP/IDL) from your home country before you arrive in Aus. This is valid for 12 months. If your licence does not have a photo, you may also need an International Driving Permit to hire a car.

> ## 🛣️ DRIVE ON THE LEFT!!!
> In Australia you drive on the **LEFT** side of the road and vehicles are right-hand drive.
> If you are used to driving on the right, ask a passenger to remind you each time you get in your vehicle.

Can I use my International Driving Licence for my whole trip?

In most states, if you have a temporary visa you can use your International Driving Licence to hire and drive a vehicle for the duration of your time in Australia. The exception to this rule is in the Northern Territory, that requires you to apply for an NT driving licence once you have been in the state for 3 months. If your international driving licence expires you must apply for a state specific licence. If you hold a permanent visa you generally have 3 months in which to convert your licence to an Australian one before your international licence becomes invalid.

How old do I need to be to hire a campervan?

The minimum age is generally 21. There are a few companies that have now lowered minimum age to 18, but be aware, anyone under 21 will often have to pay a big additional surcharge regardless of the length of hire.

> **It is legal to drive in thongs (flip flops), heels or barefoot.**
> Although this is totally legal, the safest thing to do if you are wearing thongs or heels is remove them and drive barefoot.
>
> **FACT**

Getting Fuel

The majority of cars in Australia run on unleaded petrol (ULP). Most other vehicles (mainly 4WD's and trucks) use diesel, however there is an ever-growing number of electric cars. Ensure that you pre-plan your trip and know where you are going to refuel as many fuel (service) stations close at night and they can be hundreds of kilometres apart. There are currently over 630 electric car charging stations across Australia.

Roundabouts (traffic circle)

In Australia traffic on a roundabout goes CLOCK-WISE.

- If you are turning **LEFT** (first exit), approach the roundabout in the left-hand lane and signal left.
- If you are turning **RIGHT** (last exit), approach the roundabout in the right-hand lane and signal right. Signal left just before the exit you wish to take.
- If you are **GOING STRAIGHT**, approach the roundabout in either the left or right lane but do not signal. Signal left just before the exit you wish to take.

> **When approaching a roundabout, always give way to cars on your right.**
> You only have to wait for cars on your right if they enter the roundabout before you. Otherwise you may go if it is safe to do so. On smaller roundabouts you may have to give way to cars entering on your left or across from you depending on where they are exiting.
>
> **FICTION**

Overtaking

If the centre of the road has a single line that is broken/dotted, you are permitted to cross this line and overtake when it is safe to do so. If there are double lines down the centre of the road, you are only permitted to overtake if the line closest to you is broken/dotted.

Look out for WILDLIFE

Drivers need to be on the constant lookout for wildlife, especially at dawn, dusk and at night. Many vehicles hire companies in WA and NT do not allow driving after sunset, so if you do have to drive, slow down, don't get distracted and scan both sides of the road. Look out for Kangaroos, wallabies, wombats, koalas, possums, cassowaries, lizards and snakes.

Speed limits

Most built up urban areas in Australia have a speed limit of 50km/h unless signed. Outside of urban areas, NSW, QLD, VICTORIA, TAS and SA have a default speed limit of 100km/h and in WA and NT, the default speed limit is 110km/h unless there is a sign stating otherwise.

Stay in the left lane

In Australia you stay on the left of multi-lane roads unless you are overtaking. Australians generally aren't very good at this but it is still the law and can be enforced at any time.

There are no speed limits on some Northern Territory highways.

Years ago, there were sections of highway in NT with no limit but these areas now have a speed limit of 130km/h. This is 20-30km/h above all other Australian highway speed limits.

FICTION

School Zones

During school hours, you must slow your speed to 40km/h when driving through a school zone. In South Australia this speed limit is reduced to 25km/h and you must also slow down to this speed if you are near a school outside of school hours and a child is present.

FACT

It illegal to leave your car windows open

In Victoria, Queensland and New South Wales, it is illegal to leave your windows down or your car unlocked if you are more than 3 metres away from it!

Using your horn

Your horn can only be used exclusively as a way of warning other traffic of your presence or scaring off animals on the road. Anything outside of this use can be fined. This means no beeping at your mate to say hi/bye or honking to tell another driver they have irritated you!

Road Trains

Road trains (articulated trucks) in WA can be up to 50 metres long. They are extremely dangerous to overtake. If you do attempt it, be prepared for them to sway in the wind and you may also experience wind- rush as you pass that pulls your vehicle towards the road train. Just be patience.

Tolls

Around many cities, you will need to pay a toll for using certain motorways, bridges or tunnels. To pay a toll you must have a transponder in your vehicle. If you do not have one, a photo of your numberplate is automatically taken and an invoice is issued. You have between 1- 3 days to pay depending which state you are in and if you are late paying, fee escalate quickly. Many hire companies have an agreement with the toll providers that lower the cost so make sure you ask.

Mobile phones

With penalties for mobile phone use increasing in some states to a fine, plus 4 demerit points for a first offence, here are the facts you need to know;

• Learner divers and 'P Plate' drivers (provisional) are not permitted to use mobile phone whilst driving under any circumstances. This includes making hands free calls and even listening to music.

• Full licence holders can only use their mobile phone for maps and calls when driving if it is securely mounted to the vehicle, using a commercially manufactured and designed cradle or mount. The phone must not obscure the driver's view of the road.

> **You are allowed to drink alcohol in the car so long as you are under the limit**
> Whilst this was the true over 10 years ago this is definitely no longer the case. It is illegal to drive whilst drinking regardless of your blood alcohol level.
>
> **FICTION**

• Drivers are only permitted to make or answer calls without a cradle, **IF the phone can be activated without being touched**. i.e. it can be activated via voice activation or Bluetooth.

• Drivers are only permitted to hold a phone if they are passing it to a passenger. Be careful not to get distracted though as this can get you fined too. It is illegal to hold a phone even if it is on your lap.

• Texting, emailing, video messaging, using social media and taking photos are all illegal, even if your phone is correctly fitted to a cradle/mount. This includes if you are stopped at a red light or stuck in traffic.

Fog lights can be turned on during the day to make you more visible on sunny days.

Due to the angle of fog lights, if they are turned on under normal driving conditions, they can temporarily blind oncoming drivers. Only use fog lights in the fog or you may get fined.

FICTION

Seat belts
It is the responsibility of the driver to ensure that every passenger is wearing a seatbelt before you start driving. Children (up to 7) must be fitted in an approved, age appropriate child restraint.

Emergency vehicles
Australia wide, drivers are required to move out of the way of Emergency vehicles with their lights flashing **IF IT IS SAFE TO DO SO.**

BROKEN DOWN?
If you have broken down in a remote area, do not leave your vehicle as it will provide you with both shade and shelter from the ever-changing weather conditions.

You may get fined if you eat or drink whilst driving.
Although there are no laws stating that drivers can't eat at the wheel, Australia has brought in new laws regarding distracted drivers. If eating and drinking interferes with your ability to control the car you may get fined.

FACT

HAD AN ACCIDENT?

If you are involved in an accident and someone has been hurt, you must stop, call the emergency services and give assistance. There are severe penalties for leaving an accident scene. Even if no one is hurt, you must exchange details for insurance purposes.

If you find yourself in a position where you need to administer first aid, do your best and know that the law will protect you form any legal action against you.

What information do I need?
Name/ Address - Ask to see a driving licence to ensure that they are correct.
Vehicle details - Make/Model, Registration number, colour, etc
Location and Time - Take photos of the damage and take a screenshot of your location using a maps app on your phone.

Additional information that is useful;
- Drivers driving licence number
- Drivers phone number
- Insurance details-name and policy number

Its ok to ride a bike, scooter or skateboard when intoxicated

Road rules apply regardless of your mode of transport. Although penalties are higher if you chose to get behind the wheel, you may also get a fine if you are over the limit riding too. Take a taxi, UBER or bus.

FICTION

Drinking and Driving

In Australia, it is illegal to drive a vehicle if your blood alcohol level is 0.05% or higher. If you are a learner or provisional driver your level must be zero. Random road-side alcohol and drug tests by police are common.

Eating food after drinking will lower your blood alcohol levels
Eating before you start to drink will slow the rate of the alcohol reaching the bloodstream, but not after.

FICTION

What is a standard drink?
One standard drink is approximately:

SPIRITS
1 x 30ml shot/ nip

BEER
1 x POT (285ml)

LIGHT BEER
1 x CAN (375ml)

WINE
1 x SMALL GLASS (100ml)

Please note:
British pint size=568 ml
American pint size=473 ml

The general guide is;
- **Females** - a maximum of **one standard drink in the first hour and one standard drink each hour after that.**
- Males - a maximum of **two standard drinks in the first hour and one standard drink each hour after that.**

Source – police.wa.gov.au/ Traffic/Offences/Drink-driving

Please note: **'Landed in Australia' recommends that you don't drink any alcohol if you plan to drive. Alcohol affects different people in different ways and it is simply not worth the risk.**

Not sure where to park?
What do all the signs mean?

P	The number before the P indicates how many hours you can park **3P = 3 HOURS**
T or TICKET	This means you will need to purchase a ticket from a parking meter or on an App
ARROW	The arrow tells you which direction these rules apply. The rules start from the sign.
TIMES	Tells you what times these rules are enforced. Outside these times the rule does not apply

No Stopping	No stopping at any time, not even to drop someone off
No Parking	You must remain within 3 metres of your vehicle and have a time limit of 2 min after stopping
Loading Zone	For use by vans, trucks, utes and other commercial vehicles for loading/ unloading. Time limits apply
Permit Zone	Only vehicles displaying the current relevant permit issued by the governing body can park
Clearways	Only public transportation i.e. buses, taxis or minibuses can use to pick up or drop off

RANDOM STATE SPECIFIC ROAD RULES

NEW SOUTH WALES

You can be fined for not locking your car	The law specifies the car must be locked if you are more than 3 metres away from it.
It is illegal to wave out of the window	Technically true as the law states no part of your body can be outside a moving vehicle.
It is illegal to drive through a puddle and splash people who are waiting for a bus	If the people you splash aren't waiting for a bus there may be a loophole!
Immediate Licence Suspension for drug and alcohol testing	Drink drivers who are first-time, lower-range offenders will receive an immediate three-month licence suspension and fine of $603. If you end up in court, the fines are far more!
Running a yellow light	Just like running a red light, running a yellow could get you a fine and 3 demerit points.

QUEENSLAND	Drivers must give way to a 'restive horse' - 'Restive horse' means a horse that is nervous or agitated.	If the person in charge of the horse signals to you and points to the horse you must pull over and turn off your engine until there is no reasonable likelihood that the noise of the motor, or the movement of the vehicle, will aggravate the horse.
	Drivers must carry their licence with them	In Queensland, if you are stopped by the police you must be able to produce your licence and provide your name and current address or you may be fined.
VICTORIA	Speed limits are different	Victoria is extremely strict when it comes to speeding, with driver's reported being fined for going 2km/h over the limit. Hidden speed cameras can be anywhere so slow down!
	U-Turns permitted at traffic lights	Unlike most of the rest of Australia, U-Turns are permitted at traffic lights in Victoria unless there is a sign specifically forbidding it.

RANDOM STATE SPECIFIC ROAD RULES

TASMANIA	Keep left unless overtaking is permitted	This rule applies to multi-lane roads where the speed limit is over 80km/h.
	A single unbroken line is the same as double unbroken lines in other states	Tasmania replaces all double unbroken lines with single ones but the same 'no overtaking' rule applies.
	Zip Merge Rule	In Tasmania, if 2 lanes are merging into 1, the car that is in front has right of way regardless of what lane they are in.
AUSTRALIAN CAPITAL TERRITORY	Immediate Licence Suspension for drug and alcohol testing	If you fail or refuse to take a drug or alcohol test you may be faced with an immediate license suspension.

WESTERN AUSTRALIA	Speed cameras on tripods	Generally, speed cameras in WA are mounted on small tripods which are notoriously hard to see.
NORTHERN TERRITORY	Speed limits on Highways can differ	Some sections of highway in NT have a speed limit of 130km/h. This is 20km/h over the highway speed limits in other states.
SOUTH AUSTRALIA	25km/h speed limit when passing emergency vehicles	In 2014 South Australia changed the speed limit when passing through an 'Emergency Service Speed Zone' from 40km/h to 25km/h.

Driving in Melbourne

If you plan to drive in Melbourne there are 2 additional road rules that you need to know to avoid a potentially serious accident. These rules are for:

- Hook Turns
- Driving with Trams

In this information, an intersection is where 2 roads cross completely.

All the information below is taken directly from:
Government, V. (2019, Febuary 28). vicroads.vic.gov.au. Retrieved from vicroads.vic.gov.au/safety-and-road-rules/road-rules/information-for-tourists-about-victorian-road-rules

Hook turns

If you are from interstate or overseas it is likely that a 'hook turn' is very foreign to you. At some intersections in Melbourne where trams operate, to turn right you must do a 'hook turn'. These intersections are clearly marked, with a sign hanging overhead or on the side of the road.

If turning right at an intersection with traffic lights and a 'Right Turn from Left Only' hook turn sign, you must make a hook turn so as not to delay trams.

To do a hook turn you must:

1. Approach and enter the intersection from the left lane and indicate that you are turning right.

2. Move forward to the far left side of the intersection, keeping clear of the pedestrian crossings.

3. Remain stopped until the traffic lights on the road you are turning into have changed to green.

4. Turn right.

RIGHT TURN
FROM LEFT
ONLY

Driving with Trams

There are several rules about driving in Melbourne that relate to trams:

Giving way to trams
When driving, you must:
- not move into the path of an approaching tram
- give way to a tram moving into or through a roundabout.

Safety zones
You must drive to the left of a safety zone, and slowly enough to be able to stop and avoid pedestrians.

Overtaking a Tram
You may only overtake a tram on the left.
Do not drive past the rear of a tram stopped at a tram stop (where there is no safety zone, dividing strip or traffic island)

Tram that is stopping
You must stop level with the rear of the tram and wait for people to get on and off and for the tram doors to be closed before proceeding.
If the tram doors are open and the road is clear of pedestrians then you may only drive past if directed to do so by a uniformed tram employee and provided that you drive at 10 km/h or less.
If you are already passing when the tram stops, you must give way to pedestrians on the road between the tram and the far left side of the road.

Raised dividing strips
You are not allowed to drive over raised dividing strips which run beside some tram tracks
You can drive through a break in the dividing strips but you must give way to any trams or vehicles travelling on the road you are entering.

Tramways
You are not allowed to drive in a tramway, unless you need to avoid an obstacle. Tramways have:
- overhead 'Tram Only' signs that show a picture of a tram and the word 'ONLY'
- two solid yellow lines or raised dividing strips beside the tram tracks.

Tram lanes
Tram lanes are designated by a tram lane sign (which may indicate hours of operation) and a continuous yellow line. You must not drive in a tram lane during the times it is operational, except for up to 50 metres before turning, so long as they do not obstruct the progress of a tram.

Beach Driving

Beach Driving can be EXTREMELY FUN,
but it can also be EXTREMELY DANGEROUS!

To have a great trip, please take safety seriously and allow lots of extra time. The rules are there for a very good reason. Emergency help can be hours away and if you are in remote areas you may not even have phone signal.

ROAD RULES

Police patrol beaches so ensure that you stick to the rules;

1. Driver must have a valid driving licence and carry it with them

2. Vehicles must be registered

3. It is the driver's responsibility to ensure all occupants are wearing seatbelts when the car is moving

4. Traffic is two-way. Keep to the left of oncoming vehicles

5. Do not drink or use illegal drugs and drive

6. Do not drive tired or hungover

7. Obey all speed limits

8. Travel at least 3 car lengths from the vehicle in front

9. It is illegal to travel outside of a vehicle which includes hanging out of windows

BE PREPARED

1. Check the weather and understand the tide times – Travel at low tide or within 2 hours either side of low tide. Bad weather can come in fast and can create huge swells that change everything.

2. Check beach and track condition reports for the area and ask questions to see if there are any areas you should avoid.

3. Only take a 4WD that has high clearance with low range gear selection and make sure that it is capable of dealing with difficult conditions. Your transmission and differentials will have to work hard in the sand so make sure they have been recently serviced.

> **SUV (Sport Utility Vehicles) and AWD (All-Wheel-Drive vehicles) are not suitable for beach driving.**

4. Have a full kit of good quality, working recovery gear (including spare tyres) and if hiring a 4WD get good instructions and check their safety gear: it could save your vehicle or even your life. Always carry a tyre pressure gauge and pump to inflate or deflate your tyres depending on driving conditions.

5. Do not overload your vehicle and remember to consider the weight of the passengers as part of the load. Pack evenly, putting heavy items low down to avoid your vehicle from toppling over when you turn.

6. If you are new to sand driving then either take some lessons first or have an experienced driver come with you. Always travel with another vehicle in remote areas in case you get in trouble and always let a responsible person know where you are and what time you will be returning.

WHAT SHOULD I BRING?

1. Working, accurate tyre pressure gauge
2. Portable air compressor or pump to reinflate tyres
3. Traction mats/ Traction Aids
4. Shovel
5. Well stocked first aid kit
6. Extra drinking water
7. Spare fuel
8. Food
9. Spare tyres

Beach Driving Permits

Ensure you have a valid vehicle permit for those areas where a permit is required. For beach driving in NSW or QLD, permits can be purchase using the details below. For all other States, search online for the beach name and contact the relevant governing body so that you aren't fined.

You can ride in the back of a UTE (pickup) or in the boot of a car if you are on the beach. On the beach, all road rules apply. It is illegal to be in any moving vehicle without a correctly fitted seatbelt. It is the driver's responsibility to make sure all passengers wearing seatbelts before they start driving.

FICTION

QLD
parks.des.qld.gov.au/management/managed-areas/recreation/vehicle-permits

NSW
Search for 'NSW Beach permits' and select your chosen NSW area.

DINGOS – PEOPLE INTERACTION

It is an offence to feed a dingo, attract it using food or food waste, or disturb it anywhere on Fraser Island. Penalties apply.

Dingos are wild animals and hunt their prey. Attracting and feeding dingoes make the animals less fearful of people and they become dependent on hand-outs. Hunting skills decline and they may then become aggressive towards people who don't feed them.

Let them be wild. Ensure all food and rubbish is securely locked away and always take photos from a distance.

Dingoes have bitten visitors and are capable of killing people. Some dingoes have become so high-risk that they have to be euthanised, sadly for habits learnt from people.

HAZARDS

Sand diving needs your total concentration and there are many hazards that even the most experienced road driver wouldn't be accustomed to. Be prepared, take your time, take regular breaks and don't get distracted!

If you feel threatened by a dingo:

1 STAND UP
to your full height

2 FACE
the dingo

3 FOLD YOUR ARMS
and keep eye contact

4 BACK AWAY
calmly

5 STAND BACK TO BACK
if in pairs

6 CALL FOR HELP
confidently

7 DO NOT RUN
or wave your arms.

PROTECT THE SAND DUNES

Many of the beaches around Australia are backed by vegetated sand dunes. These dunes have a very important role to play in protecting the beaches. When there are cyclones, storms or strong winds, they absorb a lot of the energy produced by the damaging waves that can erode the beaches. When erosion does occur, they create reservoirs of sand that help nourish and repair. The vegetation on the dunes trap the sand that is blown from the beach and stops it being blown inland and lost. Even walking on the sand dunes can destroy the plants and weaken the dunes so it is extremely important that you **NEVER** drive a vehicle over sand dunes (fines apply), nor should vehicles be driven on sandy areas along the debris or drift lines as these are potential sites for the formation of new dunes. Ensure that you only enter and exit the beach at the designated points.

HELP! - I'M BOGGED IN THE SOFT SAND!

If you have lost forward momentum in soft sand **STOP!!!** *Then follow these 7 steps;*

1. Do not continue to spin your wheels or you will get bogged even deeper.

2. Turn your engine off.

3. Put your vehicle in gear or PARK for automatic cars.

4. Put your handbrake on.

5. Dig the mounded sand from **BEHIND** your tyres using a shovel, your hands or traction mats.

6. Ensure the ends of the traction mats are wedged firmly under your tyres.

7. Keep bystanders clear and reverse slowly until your vehicle is on solid sand.

RECOVERING A VEHICLE

Using snatch straps and tow ropes to recover vehicles can be very dangerous in sand and should definitely not be attempted unless you are a trained operator using the appropriate safety rated equipment. Rangers are not allowed to assist in this type of recovery because of the risk involved but they may be able to suggest a towing service (very $$$$) or help you with the steps for using your traction mats. *Remember to watch the tide times and never risk your own safety to save a car.*

HELPFUL HINTS

Drive on the harder sand between the waterline and the high tide mark for the firmest surface.

Reduce your tyre pressure when driving on soft sand using a pressure gauge, to increase traction but keep within the manufacturer's specifications as reduced tyre pressure will affect your vehicle's performance.

Do not leave any rubbish behind and help protect our wildlife by picking up any litter left by others.

Avoid sharp turns, sudden braking, high-speeds and driving over very rough or very soft surfaces. Tyres have been known to come off their rims and serious accidents have occurred.

Remember to re-inflate your tyres to resume speed on harder sand or surfaces.

Respect the wildlife – animals are easily disturbed. Disturbances can affect their survival and remember - it was their home first!

LICENCES &

Fishing

Not all states require fishing licences however there are restrictions on the number of fish you can keep and the size, depending on the species. Fishing licences are relatively inexpensive and are the same price whether you are a local or a tourist. Licences can be purchased from the fishing authority in each state or online. For more detailed information or to purchase a licence, visit the web address below:

Fishing Licence **Required**

New South Wales	*dpi.nsw.gov.au/fishing/recreational/recreational-fishing-fee*
Victoria	*service.vic.gov.au/find-services/outdoor-and-recreation/buy-a-victorian-recreational-fishing-licence*
Tasmania	*ifs.tas.gov.au/anglers/manage*
Western Australia	*fish.wa.gov.au/Fishing-and-Aquaculture/Recreational-Fishing/Pages/Recreational-Fishing-Licences.aspx*

No Fishing Licence **Required**

Queensland	*qld.gov.au/recreation/activities/boating-fishing/rec-fishing/rules*
South Australia	*pir.sa.gov.au/recreational_fishing*
Northern Territory	*nt.gov.au/marine/recreational-fishing/rules/about-recreational-fishing*
Australian Capital Territory (ACT)	*environment.act.gov.au/nature-conservation/fish/recreational-fishing-in-the-act*

PERMITS

Camping Permits

Australian National Parks are managed independently by each state authority, meaning entry fees, permits and camping costs vary across states and campsites.

Before camping in a park, forest or reserve, you must obtain a camping permit and pay your camping fees.

Most camping areas can be booked online, at an over-the-counter booking office or by phone.

Queensland	*parks.des.qld.gov.au*
New South Wales	*nationalparks.nsw.gov.au/passes-and-fees*
	environment.nsw.gov.au/questions/national-park-cost-camp
Western Australia	*parkstay-waiting.dbca.wa.gov.au*
South Australia	*parks.sa.gov.au/book-and-pay*
Australian Capital Territory (ACT)	*parks.act.gov.au/get-involved/bookings-and-permits*
Northern Territory	*parkbookings.nt.gov.au/Web*
Victoria	*parks.vic.gov.au/where-to-stay/booking-information*
Tasmania	*parks.tas.gov.au/explore-our-parks/know-before-you-go/entry-fees*

OOOEMERGENCY

Triple Zero (000)

The primary emergency service number

112 and 106

Secondary emergency service numbers*

> The App you'd be lost without...
>
> **EMERGENCY+**

When to call (000)?

For Emergency help during storms, tsunamis, floods, call the **State Emergency Services (SES)**

132 500

For **Non-Urgent** Police assistance

131 444

Triple Zero (000) should **ONLY** be called in life threatening or time critical situations when an urgent response is required from:

Police
Fire and Rescue
Ambulance

What will happen when I call?

The operator will ask you which emergency service you require. You do not need to explain the situation to the switchboard operator. Just let them know which service you require and they will connect you to the relevant emergency service operator.

Will the operator know where I am calling from?

• If you call (000) from a landline, the operator will be able to see your location on screen but you will still need to confirm what town and state you are calling from.

• If you call (000) from a mobile phone service, the operator will not know where you are calling from. You will need to provide as much information as possible about where you are.

See appendix pg 80

TIPS for helping emergency services find you

• Provide the street number, street name, nearest cross street and the area.

• If you call while travelling, state the direction you are travelling, the last motorway exit, or town you passed and a description of the vehicle you're in.

REMEMBER...

- *STAY CALM*
- *CLEARLY ANSWER THE OPERATORS QUESTIONS*
- *STAY ON THE LINE*
- *DO NOT HANG UP UNTIL YOU ARE TOLD TO DO SO*

Common questions that are asked when calling an AMBULANCE:

- What's the **address** of the emergency?
- What is the **problem**?
- **How many people** are injured?
- **How old** is the injured person?
- What is the person's **gender**?
- Is the person **conscious**?
- Is the person **breathing**?
- Do you know of any **medical history**?

The operator may give you first-aid advice while the ambulance is on its way.

AMBULANCE

What if I have difficulty speaking English?

If you have difficulty speaking English, you can ask for an interpreter once you have been transferred to the emergency service you requested.

You will <u>not</u> have to pay for the interpreter.

Need a **Doctor** or **Pharmacy** that's **open** now?

Visit the site below and simply enter your suburb, postcode or use your current location to receive a list of the nearest services and whether they are open now.

➡️ *healthdirect.gov.au/after-hours-gp-helpline*

After- Hours GP (doctors)
FREE Helpline - healthdirect

1800 022 222
Free from landlines and some mobile phone services

What is the After- Hours GP Helpline for?
- It gives you access to **medical advice** outside regular doctors opening hours

What assistance can the After- Hours Helpline provide?
- An assessment of your health issue by a qualified nurse
- A GP (doctor) call back within 15 mins to 1 hour depending on the urgency of your health issue *(if required)*
- A care advice summary sent to you via SMS or email detailing the advice given *(if required)*

- A summary sent to your regular doctor's practice over night so that they have a record of the call the next day *(if required)*
- A summary uploaded to your *'My Health Record'*, if you have one.

NOTE:

This is an advice line only and a doctor will not come out to you. If you urgently require a doctor you will be advised to call 000 or visit the Emergency department at your local hospital.

OPEN

Opening Hours

Within a major city
- Monday to Friday
  11pm - 7:30am
- Saturday
  from 6pm
- Sunday & Public Holidays
  all day

Outside the major cities
- Monday to Friday
  6pm - 7:30am
- Saturday
  from midday
- Sunday & Public Holidays
  all day

Bushfires & Natural Disasters

In Australia bushfires and extreme weather events pose a real and very dangerous threat to backpackers, especially through the summer months. The 2019/2020 summer generated an unprecedented number of bushfires and Australia is famous for extreme cyclones that produce high winds and torrential rain. There are numerous ways that you can access accurate and up to date information to avoid finding yourself unprepared or in an unnecessarily dangerous situation. Being prepared, knowing what to do and knowing who to contact if you find yourself in danger, is the key to having a safe backpacking experience.

Warning levels – What do they mean? *Source: Bureau of Meteorology*

Type of Danger	Danger Level	Meaning
BUSHFIRES	Advice	A fire has started. There is no immediate danger. Stay up to date in case the situation changes.
	Watch & Act	There is a heightened level of threat. Conditions are changing and you need to start taking action to protect yourself and others.
	Emergency Warning	An Emergency Warning is the highest level of Bush Fire Alert. You may be in danger and need to take action immediately. Any delay now puts your life at risk.
CYCLONES	Watch	When onset of gales is expected within 24 to 48 hours.
	Warning	When onset of gales is expected within 24 hours or gales are already occurring.
FLOODS	Minor Flooding	Causes inconvenience. Low-lying areas next to water are inundated. Minor roads may be closed and low-level bridges submerged.
	Moderate Flooding	In addition to the above, the evacuation of some houses may be required. Main traffic routes may be covered. The area of inundation is substantial in rural areas.
	Major Flooding	In addition to the above, extensive rural areas and/or urban areas are inundated. Properties and towns are likely to be isolated and major traffic routes likely to be closed. Evacuation of people from flood-affected areas may be required.

HOW TO KEEP UP TO DATE?

RADIO
ABC Radio has up to date coverage of fires and natural disasters.
To find the frequency for ABC radio in your area visit;
reception.abc.net.au
and type in your suburb.

WEBSITE
ABC Emergency has all the major events around Australia
abc.net.au/news/emergency
For more detailed information, go to your relevant state.

FACEBOOK
ABC Emergency has all the major events around Australia
ABC Emergency (+ State) i.e. ABC Emergency Queensland
For state specific information visit the following pages;

Australian Capital Territory	ACT Emergency Services Agency
	ACT State Emergency Service
Northern Territory	Northern Territory Police, Fire and Emergency Services
New South Wales	Fire and Rescue NSW
	NSW SES
Queensland	Queensland Fire and Emergency services
Tasmania	Tasmania Fire Service
	Tasmania SES
Victoria	VIC Emergency
	Victoria State Emergency Service
Western Australia	Fire & Rescue Service of Western Australia
	WA State Emergency Service

EMERGENCY Survival Plan

1. WHEN will you leave?
What danger rating will be your trigger to leave?

BE PREPARED
Taking 20 minutes to discuss and write down the answers to these questions could save your life. It will also help your friends and family to know that you are prepared!

2. WHERE will you go?
Do you know where the local emergency evacuation locations are? What is your back up plan? Consider shopping centres and cinemas etc.

3. HOW will you get there?
Do not rely on public transport or hitchhiking as part of your plan.

4. WHAT route will you take?
What is your alternative route if roads become blocked or impacted by the emergency?

5. WHAT will you take with you?
Check out our Emergency Survival Kit guide and have it packed and ready to GRAB and GO.

6. HOW will you stay informed of warnings and updates?
Check out our state based social media links and write down your local emergency radio frequency in case you are unable to access the internet.

7. WHO do you need call to and keep updated about your location and safety?
Write down names and phone numbers in case your phone runs out of battery.

Emergency Survival Kit

If you find yourself in an emergency situation you may have to leave fast. Make yourself a 'GRAB & GO' Kit so you are always prepared. Contents include:

- Emergency Survival Plan
- Phone numbers for family and friends
- Overnight bag with 2 changes of clothes – long sleeved, closed shoes and a hat to protect you
- Toiletries – incl. sanitary products, glasses, face wipes etc.
- Medication and a Basic First Aid Kit
- Important info – Passport, Visa, Driving Licence etc - either written down or on a USB
- Mobile Phone and Charger
- Torch – Battery operated
- Portable Radio – Battery operated
- Extra batteries
- Small woollen blanket
- ATM cards
- Cash/ Change for pay phones
- Water
- Non-Perishable Food items – Food that won't go off!

Remember: Do NOT rely on having phone signal or electricity to charge your mobile

Mobile Phone Alerts

If your mobile handset has recently been in contact with a mobile phone tower in a warning area, you may receive a text message. This is based on your mobile phone's last known location. There are some limitations which may prevent you from receiving a message - such as if your mobile is switched off or if there is no coverage in your area.

Informing overseas *relatives* you are safe and registering for updates visit;

register.redcross.org.au

Contact your Consulate

Consular assistance
is help and advice provided by the diplomatic agents of a country to citizens of that country who are living or traveling overseas.

Wikipedia contributors. "Consular assistance." Wikipedia, The Free Encyclopedia. Date of last revision, 26 January 2023.

Such assistance may take the form of:

- Provision of replacement travel documents

- Help during crises, such as civil unrest and natural or global disasters

- Advice and support in the case of accident, serious illness or death

- Providing a list of local doctors and lawyers for medical and/or legal issues.

- Advise and support to victims of serious crime overseas, and arranging for next-of-kin to be informed.

- Liaison with local police officials in the case of nationals abducted or missing overseas

- Loans to distressed travelers

Call the helpline opposite for a full list of assistance

To find your local consulate visit;

protocol.dfat.gov.au/Public/ConsulatesInAustralia

*Simply select your home country and you will find the address,
contact number and opening times for your consulate in each State.*

Such assistance commonly does not extend to:

- Storing luggage or valuables
- Intervening in commercial disputes on behalf of their nationals
- Providing travel agency, banking, or postal services
- Money changing
- Translation and interpreting services
- Legal advice or advocacy
- Negotiation of special treatment, bail, or early release from prison
- Criminal investigation
- Employment services

Can't get online?

Call the Australian Government
24-hour consular assistance on;

1300 555 135

Select *option 6* and they will look up
the direct number for your local consular for you.

National Crisis Numbers

24 hours a day, seven days a week (24/7)

Lifeline **13 11 14** Crisis Support

Kids Helpline **1800 551 800** for young people 5-25 years

1800RESPECT **1800 737 732** Sexual Assault & Domestic Violence Helpline

MensLine Australia **1300 78 99 78** for men of any age

Suicide Call Back Service **1300 659 467**

These phone lines are available to anyone in Australia 24/7, and are free or provided at the cost of a local call *(some charges may apply to mobile users).*

State-based mental health crisis numbers (24/7)

ACT
1800 629 354
*Mental Health
Triage Service*

NSW
1800 011 511
*Mental Health
Line*

NT
08 8999 4988
*Top End Mental
Health Service*

QLD
13 43 25 84
13 HEALTH

SA
13 14 65
*Mental Health
Assessment & Crisis
Intervention Service*

TAS
1800 332 388
*Mental Health
Services Helpline*

VIC
1300 651 251
*Suicide
Help Line*

WA
800 676 822
*Mental Health
Emergency Response
Line*

*Let's talk about
Mental Health*

Australian Public Holidays 2023-2024

DATE	DAY	HOLIDAY	STATE	
1 May	Mon	Labour Day	QLD	
		May Day	NT	
5 May	Fri	AGFEST	TAS	
29 May	Mon	Reconciliation Day	ACT	
5 Jun	Mon	Western Australia Day	WA	
12 Jun	Mon	King's Birthday	National except QLD & WA	
7 Jul	Fri	Alice Springs Show Day	NT	
14 Jul	Fir	Tennant Creek Show Day	NT	
21 Jul	Fri	Katherine Show Day	NT	
28 Jul	Fri	Darwin Show Day	NT	
7 Aug	Mon	Picnic Day	NT	
16 Aug	Wed	Ekka Wednesday	QLD	
18 Aug	Fri	Borroloola Show Day	NT	
25 Sep	Mon	King's Birthday	WA	

TBA		AFL Grand Final Friday	VIC
2 Oct	Mon	Labour Day	ACT, NSW, SA
	Fri	King's Birthday	QLD
6 Oct	Thu	Burnie Show	TAS
12 Oct	Fri	Royal Launceston Show	TAS
20 Oct	Thu	Flinders Island Show	TAS
26 Oct	Mon	Royal Hobart Show	TAS
6 Nov	Tue	Recreation Day	TAS
7 Nov	Fri	Melbourne Cup Day	VIC
1 Dec	Sun	Devonport Show	TAS
24 Dec	Mov	Christmas Eve	NT, QLD & SA
25 Dec		Christmas Day	National
26 Dec	Tue	Boxing Day	National except SA
	Sun	Proclamation Day	SA
31 Dec		New Year's Eve	NT, SA

Date	Day	Holiday	Region
1 Jan	Mon	New Year's Day	National
10 Jan	Wed	Devonport Cup	TAS
26 Jan	Fri	Australia Day	National
12 Feb	Mon	Royal Hobart Regatta	TAS
28 Feb	Wed	Launceston Cup	TAS
4 Mar	Mon	Labour Day	WA
5 Mar	Tue	King Island Show	TAS
11 Mar	Mon	Canberra Day	ACT
		Eight Hours Day	TAS
		Labour Day	VIC
		Adelaide Cup Day	SA
29 Mar	Fri	Good Friday	National
30 Mar	Sat	Day following Good Friday	National except TAS & WA
31 Mar	Sun	Easter Sunday	National except NT, SA & TAS
1 Apr	Mon	Easter Monday	National
2 Apr	Tue	Easter Tuesday	TAS

25 Apr	Thu	Anzac Day	National
3 May	Fri	AGFEST	TAS
6 May	Mon	Labour Day	QLD
		May Day	NT
27 May	Mon	Reconciliation Day	ACT
3 Jun	Mon	Western Australia Day	WA
10 Jun	Mon	King's Birthday	National except QLD & WA
5 Jul	Fri	Alice Springs Show Day	NT
12 Jul	Fri	Tennant Greek Show Day	NT
19 Jul	Fri	Katherine Show Day	NT
26 Jul	Fri	Darwin Show Day	NT
5 Aug	Mon	Picnic Day	DT
14 Aug	Wed	Ekka Wednesday	QLD - Brisbane only
16 Aug	Fri	Borroloola Show Day	NT
23 Sep	Mon	King's Birthday	WA
TBA		AFL Grand Final Friday	VIC

APPENDIX

112 *is the International Standard Emergency number.*
- *112 can only be called by a mobile device and will redirect you to 000.*
- 112 DOES NOT connect via satellite which is a common misconception.

*Telstra is responsible for the service which answers calls to the emergency service numbers Triple Zero (000) and 112 (European Emergency Number Association) and transfers them, with relevant associated information, to the requested emergency service organisation.

**106 *is for people who are deaf or hearing impaired.*
106 can only be used by people with a TTY/textphone or a computer with terminal software (TTY imitation software) and a modem.

106 calls are given priority over other calls handled by the National Relay Service.
106 is a toll-free number. It is not possible to SMS this number.

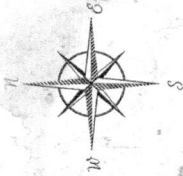

Disclaimer

The author and publisher of this book have made every effort to ensure that the information in this book is accurate and true at the time of printing. All information and recommendations are made without guarantee.
The author and publisher disclaim any liability connected to this information, to any party, for loss, damage or disruption caused by errors or omissions, regardless of cause.

© 2023 Landed in: Emma Thompson
First Edition 2023

All rights reserved. This book or parts thereof may not be reproduced in any form, stored in any retrieval system or transmitted in any form by any means - electronic, mechanical, photocopy, recording, or otherwise - without prior written permission of the publisher.
For permission requests,
email the publisher:
landedinaustralia@gmail.com

The name Landed in® is a trademark of the Landed in company.

Book design and layout by Kiki Patrali
Cover Illustration © 2023 JKerrigan

Acknowledgements

Landed in Australia would like to thank the following people for their support in making this book a reality;

Amelie Fritz – without your encouragement and support, this book would never have been started. Thank you, my friend.

Tony and Noreen Thorn – I cannot thank you enough for the advice and help you have given me throughout this entire process. Thank you from the bottom of my heart.

The incredible Lizzie – You are and always will be my inspiration. This book is for us. I am so proud of you and love you with every fragment of my being.

Charlotte Speck, you have made this book happen. Your support and encouragement is endless.

Joe Milne – thank you for your friendship and support. You are a backpacking guru and an endless source of knowledge.

Kiki Patrali - your patience and help throughout the project has been amazing. Thank you for everything you have done.

The family and friends who supported my crowd funding project. Thank you for believing in this project;

Debby and Tim Sewter, Tyla and Jed Elmer,
Olivia Rios and Tyrone Cooney, Jan and Noel Goldsworthy,
Bronwyn and Andrew Huckle, Philip and Suzanne Thorn,
Layne, Nate and Billie Butt, Sandra Allan-Kalkman,
Kay Parslow.

Printed in Great Britain
by Amazon

28978617R00050